Maria Tallchief

A Crowell Biography
By Tobi Tobias

Maria Tallchief

Illustrated by Michael Hampshire

THOMAS Y. CROWELL COMPANY, NEW YORK

CROWELL BIOGRAPHIES
Edited by Susan Bartlett Weber

LEONARD BERNSTEIN
by Molly Cone

WILT CHAMBERLAIN
by Kenneth Rudeen

CESAR CHAVEZ
by Ruth Franchere

SAMUEL CLEMENS
by Charles Michael Daugherty

CHARLES DREW
by Roland Bertol

ELEANOR ROOSEVELT
by Jane Goodsell

MARIA TALLCHIEF
by Tobi Tobias

JIM THORPE
by Thomas Fall

MALCOLM X
by Arnold Adoff

Manufactured in the United States of America

L.C. Card 77-87159

ISBN 0-690-51828-5   ISBN 0-690-51829-3 (LB)

3   4   5   6   7   8   9   10

Maria Tallchief

A CROWELL BIOGRAPHY

In the Osage Indian language, *Ki He Kah Stah* means "the tall chiefs." America's greatest ballerina comes from the family with this name. Maria Tallchief was born on January 24, 1925, in Fairfax, Oklahoma. Fairfax is a sleepy, small town on the Osage reservation in the southwest of the United States.

Her father, Alexander Tallchief, was a full-blooded Osage, and her grandfather, Peter Big Heart, had been chief of the tribe. Her mother, Ruth Porter Tallchief, came from Scottish and Irish people. She was given the name Elizabeth Marie Tallchief. Her family and friends called her Betty Marie.

As a child, Betty Marie liked to watch the dancing of the Osage tribe. But she saw these

Indian ceremonies just on special occasions. The Osages had given up many of their old customs to live the way most other Americans do.

In Fairfax, the Tallchief family owned a big, brick house on a hill. Betty Marie's father was an easygoing man. He did not have to work at a regular job. Oil had been discovered on the Osage reservation and the Indians received money for it. Mr. Tallchief took care of his family with his share of this money. He loved the outdoors and a comfortable, easy life. Gerald, Betty Marie's older brother, was just like him.

Mrs. Tallchief was different. She was strict and full of energy. She had great plans for Betty Marie and for her other daughter, Marjorie, who was two years younger. She wanted them to study music and dancing. And she expected them to work hard at everything they did.

When Betty Marie was three years old, she could pick out a tune on the family piano. Mrs. Tallchief decided that her daughter should take piano lessons. Betty Marie learned music quickly and easily. Mrs. Tallchief hoped that she would become a pianist when she grew up. She dreamed that one day Betty Marie would play in concerts all over the world.

By the time she was four, Betty Marie was dancing too. She took ballet lessons from a teacher who came to Fairfax once a week. This teacher did not realize that ballet dancing should be taught slowly and carefully. All she could see was

4

that Betty Marie was a clever girl with a strong body. So she showed her how to jump and leap and spin like a circus acrobat. She even put her in toe shoes and taught her to dance on the points of her toes.

Betty Marie was dancing for audiences in Fairfax when she was five. For one of these performances she wore a red, white, and blue costume. Her music was "The Stars and Stripes Forever." Waving an American flag, she whirled round and round, without stopping, on the tips of her toes.

Betty Marie was much too young for the showy, difficult work her teacher gave her. She was very lucky that her body wasn't hurt by it.

Soon Marjorie began taking lessons and performing with her sister. Mrs. Tallchief wanted to move to a big city where the girls could find better music and dancing teachers. Her choice was Los Angeles, California. Mr. Tallchief liked the idea. In California's sunshine, he said, he could play golf all year long.

When Betty Marie was eight, her family rented a large house in Los Angeles. At first she felt strange and lonely in her new home. She was glad to settle down to the things she knew best—school, music, and dancing.

The sisters went to a fine teacher, Ernest Belcher, for ballet lessons. But the first time Betty Marie danced for Mr. Belcher, he was horrified.

"If you really want to dance," he said, "you will have to start all over again from the beginning. No toe shoes, no fancy tricks, no performing. I'm surprised that your back and feet haven't been ruined by all this nonsense."

Betty Marie felt very disappointed and sad. But she was used to doing as she was told. She was an obedient child, who always tried to please her mother and her teachers. Betty Marie wasn't afraid of any amount of hard work, either. And

she loved to dance. So she began again, this time the right way, with the simplest exercises and steps.

Mrs. Tallchief still wanted her daughter to become a concert pianist. She felt that dancing was wonderful, just as long as it didn't keep Betty Marie away from her music. Betty Marie tried to be perfect in both. Every day she practiced the piano for several hours and went to a two-hour ballet class.

Betty Marie did well in her schoolwork too. She even found time to have fun with her friends. At home her mother taught her to cook and sew. But she had no time for dreaming, no time for just doing nothing.

To celebrate her twelfth birthday, Betty Marie gave a concert. For the first half she played the piano, and for the second half she danced. That concert, she said, showed how she felt inside. She was split in half between the two things she loved most. One day she would have to choose between them.

At fifteen Betty Marie was going to high school. Her favorite subject was writing. Once she wrote about deciding between music and dancing. She was also performing at the piano. And she was studying ballet with the great Russian teacher, Mme. Bronislava Nijinska.

Mme. Nijinska was also a choreographer—
a person who makes up dances. She gave Betty
Marie a leading part in one of her ballets. The
performance took place before an enormous
audience. As she danced, Betty Marie felt strong
and free. Afterward everyone told her how well
she had done. Now she realized what she wanted
more than anything else. It was to be a dancer.

Betty Marie grew to be tall and slim, with a
lovely, strong body. Her face was beautiful. She

had olive skin, mysterious dark eyes, high cheek-bones, a wide, well-shaped mouth, and a cloud of dark hair. She was a quiet, serious girl. And even more than most dancers, she was a hard worker.

When she was seventeen, Betty Marie finished high school. Her mother understood how much she wanted to dance. She allowed her to go to New York City. Many important dance groups work in New York. There Betty Marie hoped to find a job in a ballet company.

When she arrived in New York, Betty Marie felt a little lost. She knew some dancers there, but they were all busy with their own jobs. So

she went to Sergei Denham, the director of the famous Ballet Russe de Monte Carlo. Mr. Denham had seen and liked her dancing when she was a student in California. Now he said he would try her out in his company.

Betty Marie went on tour with the Ballet Russe. The company traveled from city to city, giving performances. Betty Marie danced so well that people began to notice her. Soon she was given some solo parts.

Ballet life was often hard, though, and Betty Marie was sometimes unhappy. She kept to herself at first, and many people in the company thought she was unfriendly. Some of them were jealous, because she was doing so well. Betty Marie missed her family, too. She wrote long letters home.

Still she went on trying, working hard, and

learning. Finally Mr. Denham asked her to stay on in the company. Of course she said yes.

Then Mr. Denham decided that she should have a beautiful stage name. So Betty Marie became Maria. But she refused to change Tallchief. She was proud of her American Indian name.

Maria Tallchief soon had an exciting chance. George Balanchine joined the Ballet Russe. Mr. Balanchine was a well-known choreographer. He also taught dancers. If he picked a girl out and trained her, she was sure to become a great ballerina.

Maria caught Mr. Balanchine's eye at once. Her dancing was fast and brilliant. She could jump up and beat her long, shapely legs together eight times in the air. She could turn in the air and land on the points of her strong toes. Her balance was sure. Her leaps were sharp and high. Her turns were quick and powerful.

Day after day, Mr. Balanchine worked with Maria. He was a gentle, patient teacher. But he often asked her to perform steps that seemed impossible. She tried over and over again, until she could do what he wanted. Soon she was dancing better than ever before.

After some time, Mr. Balanchine asked Maria to be his wife. She was twenty-one when they were married.

The next year Maria and her husband went to France to work with the Paris Opéra Ballet. She was the first American to dance with this company in more than a hundred years. The French people loved her. When she came out to bow, she was greeted with applause and bouquets of flowers.

Then Mr. Balanchine went back to work at his own studio in New York, the School of American Ballet. He formed a company called Ballet Society with dancers he had trained there. In time this group would grow into the New York City Ballet and become one of the best companies in the world. Maria joined this company as its leading dancer when she was twenty-two.

In the years that followed, George Balanchine made great changes in ballet dancing. He took old ballets and old steps and made them new and different. He tried out new ways of moving and new ways of making dances. Somehow everything he did seemed exactly right.

He created many wonderful ballets for his company, and especially for Maria. One of them was *Firebird*. Maria danced the part of a beautiful, wild bird with magic powers.

Mr. Balanchine set very difficult steps for her. They made the audience gasp with wonder and surprise. Maria flashed across the stage. She flew, she whirled, she slashed through space like a flaming arrow. *Firebird* proved that Maria was truly a ballerina. She was not just a fine dancer, but one of the best in the world.

Mr. Balanchine created other roles for Maria. She danced Eurydice in *Orpheus*. She was Sylvia in the *Sylvia Pas de Deux*. In *Swan Lake* she was Odette, Queen of the Swans. She was the Sugar

Plum Fairy in *The Nutcracker*. When she danced these parts, every line and movement of her body seemed perfect.

Maria was a very musical dancer, too. Her years of study at the piano taught her to love and understand music. This helped her to work well with Mr. Balanchine. Some of his greatest ballets had no story, no fancy scenery or costumes. They were just movements to music. Maria's dancing in ballets like *Serenade*, *Concerto Barocco*,

Four Temperaments, and *Symphony in C* helped to make the New York City Ballet famous.

Still Maria's life was almost all hard work. Every morning she took a long ballet class. In the afternoon she went to rehearsals, to practice with the company. When evening came, she put on

her stage make-up and costume. Carefully she did her warm-up exercises. Then she was ready for the performance.

In between she rested if she could. Her costumes were fitted. She saw reporters and photographers. They asked her questions and took her picture. And whenever she had a few minutes, Maria practiced by herself.

She had no time for anything outside of ballet. But, like most dancers, Maria loved her work.

Maria won many honors for her dancing. One came from her hometown. Thousands of people gathered in Fairfax for the celebration. Among them were the leaders of the Osage tribe, the governor of Oklahoma, and Maria's mother and father. There were speeches, songs, dancing, and feasting. The Osages wore their tribal dress and performed a special Indian ceremony. They gave Maria the title *Wa-Xthe-Thonba* and made her a princess of the Osage Indians.

Maria's ballet career was a success, but her marriage to Mr. Balanchine had become very unhappy. Like most women, she wanted to have children. Mr. Balanchine could not agree. He thought she should give her whole life to dancing. After several years their marriage ended. But finally Maria's wishes for a good family life came true. When she was thirty-one, she married Henry D. Paschen, Jr. He was an engineer who worked in Chicago. Three years later she became the mother of a little girl. She named her Elise Maria.

In her years with the New York City Ballet, Maria often went on tour with the company. Then people in places far from New York were able to see her dance. Maria traveled with other companies, too, as a guest ballerina. She danced all over the United States and in the big cities of Europe.

Working with other groups, Maria performed

some of the parts that have made ballerinas famous throughout history. She danced in ballets that the New York City company never presented. She also met new partners. They were excellent dancers and knew how to make a ballerina look her best.

Soon Maria began to see that the New York City Ballet was not the right place for her any more. A ballerina needs important starring roles. She must have the best partners. The New York City Ballet could not offer enough of these to Maria.

Sadly she realized that it was time for her to leave her company. Now, Maria told herself, she must look forward to other things.

Maria hoped that one day she and her sister would be in the same ballet company. She remembered how they had enjoyed performing together

when they were children. Marjorie became a famous dancer, but she married and moved to France. The two sisters were always friendly. But they never performed together again.

When she was thirty-five, Maria joined the American Ballet Theatre as its prima, or first, ballerina. She toured with Ballet Theatre for several years. She appeared with other companies as well. Everywhere she went, Maria was called America's greatest ballerina. But she was facing a hard question. What should she do next? What would be best for her as a dancer, and as a person?

She could go back to the New York City Ballet. But she felt she did not belong there any more. She could go on dancing with other companies, like Ballet Theatre. But these groups were almost always on tour. Maria was tired of traveling all the time. She was tired of dancing the same parts over and over again. Maria Tallchief was one of the finest dancers in the history of ballet. Yet there did not seem to be a good place for her in the ballet world.

Maria had a third choice, though. Now she turned to it. She once said, "Marriage and dancing are both very important, but it is better to take them one at a time." Maria's home was in Chicago, with her husband and her seven-year-old daughter. Mr. Paschen and Elise understood that a dancer's life often takes her away from her family. They were proud of Maria's success as a ballerina. But Maria always wished she could be with them more.

In 1966, when she was forty-one, Maria made her decision. She "hung up her toe shoes," as people in ballet say. Maria Tallchief left the world of dancing behind her and went home.

32

ABOUT THE AUTHOR

Tobi Tobias has been interested in the dance since she was very young. She began dancing when she was a teen-ager, and has studied both modern dance and ballet.

Because she lives in New York City, Mrs. Tobias has always been able to see the best dance companies perform. She watched Maria Tallchief throughout her career with the New York City Ballet. Before writing this book, Mrs. Tobias had a long talk with the famous ballerina.

Mrs. Tobias lives in Greenwich Village with her husband and their two children, John and Anne. She has written a number of stories for adults and children.

ABOUT THE ILLUSTRATOR

After a childhood in England's Yorkshire moors, Michael Hampshire studied art at the University of Leeds. He settled in the United States and later taught stage design at Marymount College in Tarrytown, New York. Mr. Hampshire is an experienced traveler, having journeyed through most of Europe, Ethiopia, the Sudan, Egypt, India, and Ceylon. He is now planning a trip to Guatemala to "poke around the jungles."

In doing the research for this biography, Michael Hampshire visited Maria Tallchief several times at her present home. He also went to Fairfax, Oklahoma, to get a first-hand look at her birthplace and childhood home.

jB
T
Tobias, Tobi
Maria Tallchief

DATE DUE			